Foreword

As Malachi points out in his book, his name is unique but not only that, he is a very special and unique young man. In this way, he is the same as everyone else – we are all unique! That uniqueness should be celebrated and that is exactly what Malachi achieves with this book.

Whilst reading a class novel (Wonder by R.J Palacio) during the third UK lockdown and learning from home, Malachi was inspired to explore and talk about his colour blindness and this led him to wanting to share his experiences with others. Malachi's book can teach us all something about colour blindness and how we can help and support others. Whilst this book provides facts and advice, the messages about understanding and celebrating difference extend far beyond colour blindness.

Malachi talks touchingly about how his colour blindness is inherited from his grandad and how this means he carries part of his grandad with him always. I have no doubt whatsoever that Grandad would be as proud of Malachi as his Stanhope Barrington family are.

Mrs Cross

(Headteacher of Stanhope Barrington C of E Primary School)

This 'little book' is dedicated to all those who have helped to share my story of colour blindness, and to colour blind people - like me!

It started out with me writing down a few thoughts about my colour blindness and sharing them with my family. With their encouragement I wrote more and more, and more and more, and ended up with what you have now in your hands - my book!

I had fun writing it and designing the font from my own handwriting. Thank you for taking the time to pick it up and read. I hope you enjoy it and that it helps you to better understand what colour blindness is and how it affects people.

Malachi

About ME!

Hello, my name is Malachi. It's quite a unique name and most people don't know how to spell it - or say it. A lot of people think that it's pronounced Mal-a-chee, but it is said Mal-a-kai. I could say the English language is very strange. It is - but Malachi isn't actually an English name. It's Hebrew and it's from the Bible - it means messenger of God.

I am nine years old, nearly ten, and I like (in no particular order): drawing, Lego, football, hiking up mountains, and playing imaginary games with my friends; Noah and Ethan.

Anyway, enough about me! Why am I writing this book, you may be asking?

Why
?

I want to raise peoples' awareness of colour blindness and help them to understand it!

I am **colour blind** – I got it from my grandad (my mum's dad) who was colour blind too.
Sadly, he died two and a half years ago.

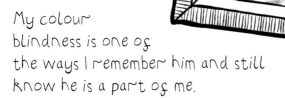

My colour blindness is one of the ways I remember him and still know he is a part of me.

What is colour blindness?

If you are colour blind, it doesn't mean you can't see anything, and it usually doesn't mean that you just see in black and white (though there are a few people who don't see any colour at all, but this is very rare).

The best way for me to describe colour blindness is that you **see** colours **differently**.

There are different types of colour blindness: red-green and blue-yellow are the main ones.

I am red-green colour blind. People think this means that I only get confused with greens and reds, but colours that also have red and green in them like orange, brown and purple, I find hard to tell the difference.

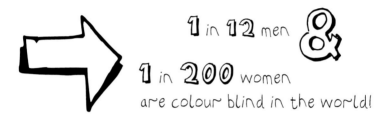

1 in 12 men & 1 in 200 women are colour blind in the world!

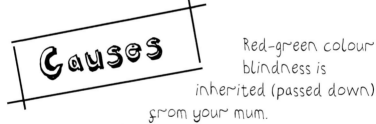

Causes

Red-green colour blindness is inherited (passed down) from your mum.
Let me tell you how - it's quite interesting. There are these weird chromosome thingies in your body which contain genes and make up how you are made. They decide what colour your hair is, eyes are, what sex you are and many other things including whether you are colour blind. We generally have 23 pairs of

chromosomes and the 23rd pair of chromosomes are either made up of an X and Y chromosome, if you are male, and two X's if you are female.

XY ≡ male   XX ≡ female

This is where it gets interesting, and a bit confusing! Let me try and explain.

The 'colour blind gene' is found only on the X chromosome.
So, for a male to be colour blind he only needs the colour blindness gene on his X chromosome. A female needs the gene to be on BOTH of her X chromosomes in order for her to be colour blind. This is why it is less common for a female to be colour blind. If she only has one colour blind gene then she is a 'carrier' (like my mum) but she won't be colour blind.

There was a 50% chance that I would be colour blind, because I could have either inherited my mum's X chromosome that had the colour blind gene on, which she had inherited from her colour blind Dad, or her X chromosome which didn't have the colour blind gene on it.

Let me draw you a diagram to explain:

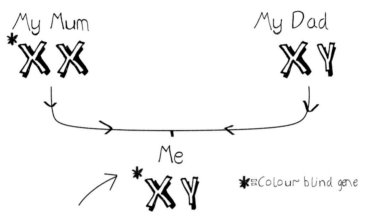

Colour blind gene passed down from my mum on the X chromosome.

For a female to be colour blind, she needs to have a Dad who is colour blind and a mum who is a 'carrier' of the colour blind gene. That way, she will inherit two chromosomes with the colour blind gene. Males can only pass down their X chromosomes to their daughters.

I read about this from a very **interesting** website about colour blindness, which has lots of information:

www.colourblindawareness.org

Check it out!

Scientists don't completely know how colour blindness is caused, but it is thought that the 3 cones in the back of the eye which *see* colour are not working in the way they should. This is all I understand as it is quite complicated!

How did I find out I was colour blind?

Mum knew a bit about colour blindness because her Dad was colour blind and knew that I might be too. My Dad **suspected** that I was colour blind when he was reading to me at bedtime one night. I was about 3 years old and I was asking questions about the colours on the page.

There was a red, green and blue ball but I was confused because two of the balls looked the same colour.

I also remember, when I was about 4 or 5, my mum telling me off for picking the green strawberries and starting to eat them because they were unripe. I didn't realise that they weren't ready to eat because I find it hard to know when fruit is ripe because I can't see the different colours sometimes. I now ask before picking strawberries in the veggie patch!

If you think you are colour blind you can go to the opticians for a colour blind test. I went just before I started Reception. They said that I was a bit young to be tested but they let me look at some pictures which were made up of coloured dots with a number inside and I had to say what number I could see. I don't remember it very well; I was only just starting school, but my mum says that I wasn't able to see some of the numbers in the pictures which she was able to see.

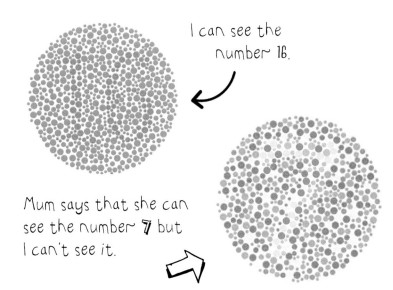

I can see the number 16.

Mum says that she can see the number 7 but I can't see it.

My experience of being colour blind

Most of the time, I like to be colour blind. Most of the time I forget. Though, sometimes when I have to colour in at school, and have to think about colours, I am reminded, and go all shy. Or sometimes I get cross when I can't join in with a game because it involves colours, or when I get given work at school which asks about colours. I guess I react in this way because I know that I'm different and don't see things like my friends do and I also feel left out or confused.

I am learning to manage these feelings, and I'm also trying to speak up for myself if I am confused by colours used – especially in the classroom.

Usually people draw in colour, but because I'm colour blind I prefer to just do shades. I LOVE drawing, but I often draw just with a pencil and shade things in. I often do this because I'm worried about what people would think of the colours I'd choose. I know that the grass is green, trees have brown trunks and the sky is blue – but when I have to choose a colour from a pot of pens and pencils, I have to think hard to work out which is which.

Imagine colouring in the grass red, when you thought it was a green colouring pencil or the sky purple because you thought it was blue!

If I do draw in colour, I usually ask people which colours are which so they don't look weird to other people - some people are more helpful than others. I also have colouring pens and pencils that have the names of the colours written on them to help me.

Sometimes I decide not to think about what other people think of the colours I use. The sky or rivers may end up purple or the grass brownish- red, but who cares?

This is a picture of a sun set I made using pastels. My Grandma really likes the colours I see, so she's quite encouraging about my art work.

My family play a game called "Yellow Car". We have to look out for yellow cars and get a point if we see them. I can see yellow - but sometimes I shout out "Yellow car!" wanting to get a point, and then someone says, "Sorry, that one was lime green". The little bit of green in the colour I can't see and so I think it's yellow.

These are some of the things I find difficult:

* Knowing if fruit is ripe - especially strawberries and bananas.

* Finding the right coloured pencil in a pot.

* Learning with colours (when teachers use colours, like in Maths and English).

* Art and colouring.

* Reading maps.

* Seeing the different teams in football matches.

* Some board games.

* Knowing if batteries are charged when red and green lights are used!

* Playing snooker.

99% of people who are colour blind have **red-green** colour blindness & red and green are the most used colours in the world!

One thing I've found annoying recently, is the Rubik's cube! My oldest sister has just learnt how to solve it - her quickest time being 47 seconds!! I find a lot of the colours difficult on the Rubik's cube. So, when I think I've solved it and get all excited, someone then says I haven't - that is annoying! **BUT** we have stuck some stickers on it now so I know the difference between the colours...I haven't solved it yet, but I'm getting there!

But like I said earlier - most of the time I don't think about being colour blind. It's just part of me, and I accept it.

If you are reading this, and are ashamed of being colour blind, it's simple: Don't be!

Sure, it can be irritating sometimes but it doesn't mean you should be ashamed of yourself. I know from experience that it only makes it worse. If you need help, ask someone.

You are unique. It only makes you, YOU! I am proud of being me because I am who I am and nobody can change that.

Whenever people ask me who I am, where I come from and what my personality is like, I usually tell them that I'm colour blind too! I don't know why; I just do it. I'm not saying I've always done that, I'm also not saying I never get cross about getting colours mixed up, or feeling left out of things or confused when colours are involved in things. I do! Though I suppose people get confused at times about different things whether they are colour blind or not. So, I suppose it's not that different being colour blind, but I also suppose it is when people don't understand how I see things! Though there are some simple things that can help me.

HELP! (Things that people can do to make things easier)

* Be KIND! If I'm not sure about the colour of something, please help me and don't make fun.

* Please don't keep asking me what colours things are! I know people are just being curious about the way I see, but it is frustrating!

* If I haven't chosen to colour something in - please DON'T ask me to make it more COLOURFUL. There is a reason I haven't chosen to use colour. Questioning me about it makes me feel uncomfortable.

* When my teachers use colours to help teach a subject, please can you label the colours for me because I might not be able to SEE them. If you print the work in black and white and can't see the differences in colour, then I won't be able to either, unless it's labelled.

✱ When playing sports, if we are split into teams, please can you think about the colours of bibs used so that I can tell the difference between them.

✱ Please believe me when I say I am struggling with something because of the colour. I don't want to cause a fuss I just want you to understand.

You can download an **APP** to find out how colour blind people see things. Search for 'colour blind simulator', in your app store on iOS or Android phones. We are all different but it will give you some understanding of what things look like to me, and how confusing it can be.

These two pictures look the same to me.

The future...

I like making electric circuits, with a circuit board a friend gave me for my birthday, but I know that I can't be an electrician, because it's pretty important to know what colour wires you are wiring up so as not to cause an explosion or get killed! I used to want to be a pilot when I was little but I know that I can't be because of my colour blindness.

If you didn't know this, and you are colour blind I hope this doesn't make you sad! I have included this information in this little book of mine so that if you are colour blind you can think of different jobs to do and don't dream of doing your 'dream' job and then find out you can't do it! My Nana told me a story of someone who wanted to join the army - and it wasn't until he went for his interviews that he was told that he couldn't be accepted because he was colour blind! It was a big shock and very disappointing for him. I don't want that to happen to you!

I think there are jobs you can now do in the army, if you are colour blind, but it's worth looking into if that's what you want to do.

So that I don't end this book on a sad note, there may be jobs that I can't do because of how I see colours, but there are things I am better at! Apparently colour blind people are better at seeing in the dark, and spotting camouflaged things because we notice the difference in textures better. I'm **very** good at finding four leafed clovers...not sure if that is because I'm colour blind or not, but my Grandad used to find them too!

Colour blindness is not something that can be cured, but it is something that you live with and grow to understand more and more.

I hope this little book of mine has helped you understand colour blindness more. Thank you for taking the time to read it! I've enjoyed writing it and I hope you've enjoyed reading it.

Malachi

Are you colour blind?

How can people help you?

OR

Do you know someone who is colour blind?

How can you help them?

Here's some space to write some of your thoughts after reading my book...

Label some pens and
pencils.
When I was little, and I
couldn't read, my mum drew
little pictures on the tops of my pens.
A plane for the RED arrows, a leaf for
GREEN, a tree for BROWN etc.

I was having difficulty in the playground playing games with my friends, because we had to collect different coloured balls. So, my mum asked my school if they had blue and yellow balls I could use because I can see those colours better.

THANK YOU'S
(Acknowledgments)

There are lots of people I'd like to thank for helping me to publish this book.

I'd first like to thank all of the people who have kindly helped to fund the making of it. If it wasn't for you then this book would not have been published!

"Thank you" to my mum. For encouraging me, helping me and for saying (at first) "I'm not sure you can publish a book!" If you tell me I can't do something I will find a way! For teaching me how to make a font from my own handwriting (very exciting), for the time she has spent sitting at her laptop getting the design for my book the way I want it, and writing to lots of people to find funding to print it and somewhere to sell it!
Thanks to Dad too, for helping mum to do this.

My sisters Rebekah and Esther, for putting up with the extra attention Mum has given me in getting this book published and for being (mostly) encouraging rather than jealous. I know Esther will, sometime, publish a book too - you are a great fiction writer. Bekah, I love the way you have been excited about my book and telling your friends and teachers about it, and helping them to understand colour blindness.

Mrs Cross for proof reading (including a GPS 'lesson' in the Easter holidays over the phone!) and for writing the foreword which made my mum cry (sad and happy tears). Also, to Miss Hepple for proof reading, and trying to make my learning in the class room easier in school, when colours are involved.

For friends and family (near and far) for reading the drafts of this book and for their helpful and encouraging comments.

For the kind words that Georgina Durrant and Michael Surr wrote about my book, that are on the back of my book cover - Thank you.

Wow! That's a lot of people. A B I G thank you to you all for believing in me.